ABOUT THE AUTHOR

Allegra Huston is the author of two highly acclaimed books, *Love Child: A Memoir of Family Lost and Found* and the novel *Say My Name* (*A Stolen Summer* in paperback), the DailyOm course "Forgiveness Through Writing" and numerous magazine and newspaper articles. She co-wrote the companion volume to this book, *How to Read for an Audience*. For over 30 years she has worked as an editor for major publishing houses in London and New York, including six years as Editorial Director of Weidenfeld & Nicolson, London, and seven years on the editorial team of the international art and culture magazine *Garage*. Authors she has worked with include two Nobel Prize winners, three Booker Prize winners, Sir James Goldsmith, and Jane Goodall.

Allegra spent two years as development consultant for the British film company Pathé and wrote and produced the award-winning short film *Good Luck, Mr. Gorski*. She has conducted creative writing workshops for the University of Oklahoma, the National University of Ireland, Galway, the Taos Writers Conference and the UK's prestigious Arvon Foundation. She holds a First Class Honours degree in English Language and Literature from Hertford College, Oxford. Please visit allegrahuston.com.

> *"I've experienced the editing process from both sides—as an editor and as an author—and those experiences have ranged from thrilling to devastating. I've learned for myself what works and what doesn't. Following these simple principles will save both you and the writer a lot of upset, confusion and miscommunication."*

Twice 5 Miles Guides
the stuff nobody teaches you

Also in this series
How to Read for an Audience

forthcoming titles
How to Teach a Workshop
How to Make a Speech
How to Tell a Story
How to Manage a Project
How to Start a Business
How to Organize a Collection
How to Sell Your Home
How to Work with a Model
How to Work with a Gallery

"I've taught for years, but the lessons in *How to Edit and Be Edited* are still very useful for those of us who teach or edit a lot. It is also an indispensable tool for students in terms of learning how to respond to fellow writers in a workshop setting. This is a very valuable book."

— Sue William Silverman, novelist and memoirist, faculty member at Vermont College of Fine Arts

"As a first-time author with a major publishing house, I feared the editing process would be a cross between a tax audit and exploratory surgery. Fortune smiled upon me when my manuscript was edited by Allegra Huston, for it became an inspirational conversation between a novice and a consummate professional with decades of experience as an editor and, more importantly, as a writer herself. What *The Elements of Style* is for writers, this slim, information-packed volume will be for editors in all creative fields."

— Brian Keating, author of *Losing the Nobel Prize* and Professor of Cosmology at the University of California, San Diego

"*How to Read for an Audience* and *How to Edit and Be Edited* should be required reading for all writers and editors, as well as all creative writing teachers and students. Both books are bursting with outstanding insights and fresh ideas. And as a bonus, they're written in prose so accomplished and excellent, they're a lesson in itself on how to write a brilliant writing guide. Whether you're a newbie beginner or a well-seasoned pro, these books will make you a better performer, editor, and writer."

— Kate Christensen, PEN/Faulkner Award-winning novelist and former teacher at Iowa Writers Workshop

"These first two Twice 5 Miles guides, on reading aloud and on editing and being edited are deft, clear and charming, without a wasted word. The series, which might as well be subtitled 'things writers are too embarrassed to ask about,' promises to immediately fill a tremendous need in the lives of those who still live and die by the book."

— Jonathan Lethem, *NYT* bestselling novelist and Roy E. Disney '51 Chair of Creative Writing at Pomona College

"*How to Edit and Be Edited* is a book I would give to every editor. There is no formal training for editors—experience and example are their only guides, until now. It is a book every publishing house should press into the hands of their young editors as they set out on learning a skill that involves such subtlety, empathy, strength and understanding. It will swiftly become an indispensable handbook for editors everywhere."

— Alexandra Pringle, Editor-in-Chief, Bloomsbury Publishing

HOW TO EDIT AND BE EDITED
A Guide for Writers and Editors

Allegra Huston

Taos • London

Copyright © 2018, 2019 by Allegra Huston

All rights reserved. No part of this book may be reproduced in any form or by any electronic or mechanical means, including information storage and retrieval systems, without permission in writing from the publisher, except by a reviewer, who may quote brief passages in a review. Scanning, uploading, and elec-tronic distribution of this book or the facilitation of such without the permission of the publisher is prohibited. Please purchase only authorized electronic editions, and do not participate in or encourage electronic piracy of copyrighted materials. Your support of the author's rights is appreciated. Any member of educational institutions wishing to photocopy part or all of the work for classroom use, or anthology, should send inquiries to Twice 5 Miles, P.O. Box 2999, Taos NM 87571, or info@twice5miles.com.

ISBN 978-0-9857528-6-6 (paperback)
ISBN 978-0-9857528-7-3 (e-book)

Twice 5 Miles
P.O. Box 2999
Taos, NM 87571

twice5miles.com

Book design by Lesley Cox, FEEL Design Associates, Taos NM

Cover design by Alex Alford, Colourfield

CONTENTS

The value of editing 1
Ground rules 9
    The rookie mistake 11
    The two basic rules of editing 12
    Talking with the writer. 17

Making notes as you read 20

General issues to consider 22
    Trust 22
    Tone 25
    Pacing. 27
    Narrative line 28
    Beginnings and endings 30
    Completeness 33
    Style 34
    Excess material 35

What to look for in specific kinds of writing ... 36
    Fiction and memoir. 36
        Screenplays and stage plays 51
    Books for young readers. 52
    Nonfiction 54
        History. 54
        Polemic 55
        Science 56
        Cooking, gardening, other how-to books 57
        Self-help 58
    Magazine articles 59
    Business/nonprofit documents 59
    Poetry. 60

For professionals 60
    Book/magazine editors and literary agents. . 60
    Film/TV producers and
    development executives 67
    Business/nonprofit executives 71

For writers. 72
    Editing yourself 72
    Writing groups. 76
    Creative writing courses 77
    Finding a good editor 77
    Asking friends and family to read your work . 79

For informal readers. 83

Further reading 87

THE VALUE OF EDITING

The word "editing" covers a lot of ground. This book is not just about changing the words on the page. It is a guide for how best to frame the collaborative effort between two people—or between your creative mind and your critical mind—that is undertaken with one simple goal: to make a writer's work as good as it can possibly be.

There is an important difference between editing—sometimes called big-picture editing, content editing or development editing—and copyediting. The overlap between them is known as line editing. A copyeditor corrects spelling and punctuation, points out repetition, tautology, wordiness or lack of clarity and suggests alternatives, and fact-checks proper names and anything that looks dubious. Line editing improves the writer's prose style and storytelling, which may involve some rewriting and perhaps moving portions of text; it requires good literary judgment, but basic competency can, like copyediting, be taught. Big-picture editing is exactly what it sounds like: assessing the impact of the book as a whole on the reader, looking for weaknesses and absences (usually very hard to spot) as well as strengths that might be strengthened further.

When the editorial collaboration works at its best, ideas emerge which neither writer nor editor would have come up with on their own. Often it becomes impossible to distinguish which idea was whose.

Editing is an art as well as a skill. It requires sensitivity to both words and narrative, a sense of rhythm in language and storytelling, good general knowledge, the ability to connect emotionally and/or intellectually with the material and, most importantly, the ability to imagine the potential that a written work might achieve. Editing is also personal; what one person loves about a book, a story, a screenplay or a marketing brochure, another may hate. This is why it's so hard to teach, and why publishing courses tend not to try.

The best way to develop your judgment is to read lots of good books, magazine articles, screenplays, grant proposals or annual reports, and ask yourself why the good ones are better than the not-so-good ones. Your judgment will get stronger with experience. This book will help you along the way, by guiding you in what to look for in written work of various kinds.

All good editors follow a few common principles. Whether the writer–editor relationship is an inner dialogue or a collaboration, the same principles apply. This book elucidates those principles, which are based on what I consider to be the two basic rules of how to work with a writer, regardless of the format or subject matter, so as to get the best result from the collaboration.

Why have an editor at all? If you're working in a business context, on commission for a magazine or news source, or with a professional publishing house, editorial input is a given. If you are self-publishing, you have the choice to skip this step—as many ill-advised writers do.

Be honest with yourself, and remember that it's hard to be objective about your own work. If you really think there's no room for improvement, fine—get your work printed up and send it out into the world. But before you invest that time and money, why not make sure that it's as good as you can possibly make it?

If you're hoping to be published by a professional house or in a magazine, either printed or online, you will need to impress the agents and editors who are gatekeepers to publication. It's a competitive world out there, and you will only have one chance at each person. Usually they have far more work than the time they've got to do it in, and reading the work of writers who aren't already on their list is a low priority. They're looking for a reason to stop reading. It's foolish to waste precious opportunities with untested work.

How do you test your work in advance? By asking people whose judgment you trust to read it. And how do you identify those people? They like the books and movies you like and can discuss them intelligently, or perhaps they've impressed you with their knowledge of the subject you're writing about. And they don't bulldoze their opinions through the middle of a discussion. In other words, they have tact as well as judgment.

If you are already in an editorial job, or have been asked to read a writer's work, you can assume that your tact and judgment are valued. Congratulations! You are well on your way to being one of the most valuable assets a writer can have.

Not all writers want to be edited. Even writers who understand the value of the process may dread it, or approach it with trepidation. As a general rule, the more professional the writer, the more amenable they are to editing—but the more impatient they are with bad editing.

Writing is an undertaking that requires courage. When you face a blank screen or page and put words on it, you're creating something out of nothing. Usually, at least to begin with, it's a pale reflection of what you've imagined. Ann Patchett describes the idea of a novel as a shimmering butterfly and the written work as the butterfly pinned down: less vibrant and less beautiful. For her, as for many writers, the finished work carries a whiff of disappointment: it may be as good as we can make it, but it's never quite as wonderful as it was before it was pinned to the page.

There's something about writing that brings out a feeling of vulnerability in almost everyone. Because we know how to form letters and employ the basic rules of grammar, we feel that it ought to be straightforward to express our thoughts in words. When a reader doesn't find in those words what we hoped we'd put into them, we feel frustrated and inadequate. It's very hard not to take criticism personally.

Bad editorial technique—which emphasizes what's wrong rather than what's strong or might be strengthened—puts the writer on the defensive, which is counterproductive in many ways. Feeling criticized makes a writer hang onto what they've already written, or it makes them lose confidence in their work or their abilities, or it makes them abandon their imaginative connection with the project and turn out a hack job.

Imagination only comes out to play when it feels safe.

This book was written for anyone who will be reading written work with the goal of improving it. Perhaps you are:

- **A writer**
  Reading over your own work can be scary. Approaching the revision process with the techniques of a good editor—in which weaknesses are seen as opportunities for exploration and expansion—defangs the inner critic. You will also be giving your work to early readers for feedback, and you'll get the best results if you follow the guidelines set out in this book. Give it or lend it to your readers before they start reading.

- **A fellow writer in a writing group or course**
  You will be reading and critiquing the work of other writers, and they will be reading and critiquing yours. You can help one another enormously—or cause one another a lot of anguish. Many writers lose belief in themselves under a barrage of friendly fire. You don't want to be on either end of that kind of feedback.

- **A friend or family member of a writer**
  I will refer to you as an informal reader, since you

are not yourself a writer or editor or aspiring to be one. Your reaction is extremely valuable, as it gives the writer a sense of how an "ordinary" reader might respond. But reading the creative work of someone you know can be extremely stressful. The techniques and advice laid out in this book will help you establish easy communication, and maybe even transform a minefield into an enjoyable experience and a great gift. You will find additional advice specifically for you beginning on p. 83.

A professional editor

You'll pick up many—though maybe not all—of these skills as you go along, most likely by a sometimes painful process of trial and error. But why subject your authors to your learning process? You may figure out my two basic rules for yourself, though many editors do not, and as a result either the work suffers, or the author suffers, or both. Get a few authors together with a bottle of wine and you'll hear plenty of editor horror stories.

A film/TV executive

You have a property and you've hired a writer to adapt it. Or perhaps it's an original screenplay with potential but it's not there yet. How can you get the best out of your writer, while also fielding the demands of other team members?

- **A business or nonprofit executive**
  All businesses generate documents for both internal and external use: grant proposals, annual reports, marketing communications and so on. It's someone else's job to write this material, and your job to oversee and sign off on it. The principles in this book will give you tools to make those documents more effective.

Other kinds of editors

The editor-in-chief of a magazine is more like a curator or a battlefield commander. They set the overall direction, generate ideas, catalyze other people's creativity, lead a team. They may directly edit the work of some contributors or they may leave that task to department editors.

A senior editor at a publishing house acquires books to publish, negotiates with agents and coordinates the packaging and marketing of the book. If they have the time and the inclination they may work with an author on the text, but it's not actually integral to the job. If a book requires heavy editing, it will usually be sent out to a freelancer.

A film/video editor pieces together the footage that's been shot so as best to tell the story. Film/video editing utilizes many of the same skills as editing written material, but rarely does an editor working with the written word come in at as early a stage as

> a film editor does. In the film and TV world, the person filling the editorial role that I describe in this book is the producer or development executive, not the editor.

Most professional editors learn by doing, in a kind of apprenticeship. You begin as an editor's assistant. If you're lucky, that editor is good at what they do, able to articulate the principles by which they're working and willing to pass on their knowledge. More often they're working by what's become instinct, so they're unable to teach—and you're left to figure it out for yourself. When I started in publishing, I rummaged through the files to find editorial notes by more experienced editors. I found a copy of notes which an editor had sent to the highly respected British novelist Angela Carter, pointing out repetitions or awkward bits of phrasing and asking, "Are you happy with this?" I saw that authors responded best when they were addressed with questions rather than critical comments. In other words, with respect.

Respect means: this is not about you. This is the writer's work. Their job is to write. Your job is to reflect, query, suggest, brainstorm, focus, clarify and inspire. Not to write.

If you're editing your own work, stay in that mindset. Give your creative mind space to digest the responses of your critical mind. Let the rewriting come later.

A good editor stays out of the writer's way. That doesn't mean you're not important, even vital—but in the end it's the writer running the race, with you coaching from the sidelines. It's not about how you'd do it; it's about how they do it—and making the way they do it as strong as it can possibly be. Therefore, be open to being wrong or having your suggestions rejected. The writer's preferences may be different from yours. In the end, it's the writer's name on the cover or the byline.

(Business/nonprofit executives: you're probably thinking, no it isn't. And you're right. You have more authority than the other editors/readers I'm addressing in this book. In the end, it is your call. Even so, you'll get a better result if the writer you're working with is energetically and imaginatively on board all the way to the end of the project.)

GROUND RULES

Your starting point, when assessing a work that is not yet in its final form, should always be that flaws are not necessarily a sign of bad writing. They are signs of a non-final draft. The object now is to assess what stage the work is at and understand what needs to be done.

The contract a writer makes with a reader is to tell their story or communicate their information clearly—in other words, not to leave the reader in a state of confusion. The reader should feel a sense of satisfaction at the end: they've learned about a subject, gained a new insight into human nature, been on an emotional journey, understood a business's objectives and achievements. First and foremost, the writer needs to know whether that sense of completion has been achieved. If it has been achieved, don't take for granted that the writer knows that. Tell them so.

But before you lay your thoughts on the writer, make sure that you have a common understanding.

If you are a junior editor at a publishing house or magazine, ask the commissioning editor to introduce you to the writer as the person doing the editing. Get an idea of how much work you think the manuscript needs. If it requires heavy editing, get the blessing of the commissioning editor first, or agree how far you will go with the author.

If you are a business or film/TV executive, make it clear to the writer exactly who will be commenting on their work and what the roles of those readers are.

If you are an informal reader, the first thing to do, when you agree to read, is set your escape clause. Say to the writer, "I'll read the first 10 pages and if I'm not connecting with it I'll just stop, because obviously I'm not the right reader for you." This simple formula prevents a lot of anguish.

Before you begin reading, ask the writer whether they want your honest feedback or just some cheerleading to keep them going. If the writer hasn't thought about this yet, your question will help them understand what stage they're at. Don't let the question sound sarcastic. Either answer is legitimate. If cheerleading is what's wanted, don't tell the writer what's not working or what you don't like; focus on the positive. I don't mean you shouldn't be honest! Just keep your responses to what's good, what's working, what you like.

Whenever you read a work in progress—whether you're a publisher of some kind, a film/TV or business executive or a friend—either ask some version of this question or keep it in mind. Creating something out of nothing is hard, lonely work, and often a writer simply needs to know they're on the right track. But if the writer is on the point of sending the work out and they're still asking for cheerleading, try to convince them that this isn't wise.

The rookie mistake

Many people who find themselves in an editorial role make the same mistake. They think they're supposed to fix the book. They've identified the problems and they expend a lot of mental energy on coming up with solutions. This, of course, makes them quite attached to their solutions. The classic version of this is the film development executive who tells you to put in a car chase (yes, it's happened to me). The story is sagging, the pace is dragging: you need some excitement! In this case, the car chase solution is like a sugar hit: a rush followed by dissatisfaction. Far better to address the underlying story issues—but it's hard to do that if a car chase, or some other plastered-on idea, is occupying the center of the discussion.

Landing on a solution and sticking to it distracts both you and the writer from identifying what the problem is.

I'll talk later about what the problem might be. For now, I want to make this important point: once you've identified what isn't working, *stop there for now*.

Remember:

It's not your job to fix it!
Your job is to *help the writer* fix it.

The two basic rules of editing

We all know that there are rules of grammar, punctuation and spelling. Those come under the heading of copyediting. Big-picture editing is, as I said, a series of judgment calls. But how should those judgment calls be conveyed to the writer? I have formulated these two rules, which have stood the test of decades of working with writers from the most eminent to the most fledgling:

Rule 1. Praise
Rule 2. Ask questions

Rule 1. Praise

Too often people think being a critic means being critical. That's only part of it, and not even a necessary part. A good critic assesses what's strong ahead of what's weak—because if a work has no strengths, why should anyone care what its faults are? And if, as a reader or editor, you don't lift up those strengths, what yardstick are you measuring the rest of the writing against? And why should the writer even want to struggle on?

I believe that if you can't say what's good about a piece of writing, you have no business telling the writer what's not good about it.

Ground rules—

Praise serves different functions:

1. *It sets the tone.* A writer is much more willing to entertain your criticisms and ideas if they know that you like their work.

2. *It sets the parameters of what the book can achieve.* A pedestrian stylist is never going to write like Jane Austen—but maybe the writer is good at ingenious plotting, like Agatha Christie, or explaining difficult concepts, or mounting a convincing argument, or eliciting sympathetic emotion in the reader. Whatever the writer's strengths are, they will be stronger in some places than in others. Identify those benchmarks so the writer can set their sights on them.

3. *It sparks ideas.* When you tell a writer what you really loved—what surprised you, what moved you, what shocked you, what made you laugh, what made you see something in a new light, a turn of phrase that delighted you, the places where you absolutely couldn't stop reading—they will often see ways to deepen those responses, or play with them, or find other places in the book that chime with the section you mentioned. The writer will see ways to improve the book that you hadn't noticed, and that they themselves might not have noticed without your enthusiasm. Which leads to:

4. *It energizes the writer.* Now they're excited! They can see what the book (or script, or story) will look like when they make that change, and they're longing to get to work on it. When a writer feels that they're succeeding, they want to add to that success by improving what's less successful. A writer who feels that they're failing may

be dogged and keep at it, but inspiration is less likely to come, if it comes at all. Often the writer will simply give up.

5. *It gives the writer confidence going forward.* The chances are the writer will meet rejection along the way to publication, and beyond. Praise from a reader or editor works as both gasoline and armor.

But what if the work is really awful?

Informal readers: You did say you'd read the first 10 pages as a trial. You can stop there and say, "I didn't connect with the story, so I guess I wasn't the right reader for you."

If you continued beyond the first 10 pages, what's gone wrong? There must have been something promising, or you wouldn't have kept reading. Was it the quality of the prose? Was it the premise or the subject matter? A character that drew you in? Praise what you can, but don't tell the writer the work is terrific if it isn't. Tell them in broad terms what didn't work for you, but try not to get pulled into saying critical things you'd prefer not to say. The situation can get uncomfortable fast, so it's best to stay vague and end the conversation as quickly as possible.

You may feel that the writer is wasting their time, but this isn't your call to make. They may get better with practice, or they may be gaining benefits from writing that don't depend on its quality.

Film/TV and magazine commissions: If the script or article really is that bad, you'll probably want to find a new writer if your budget allows. If it doesn't, be realistic about what this writer is capable of and lower your sights accordingly. You have no choice but to build on this writer's strengths, so your first task is to identify what they are. The writer must have some strengths, or why are you working with them in the first place?

If you are planning to hire a new writer, think about what went wrong this time. If you think the writer simply can't write, why didn't you notice that in their writing samples? If the writer didn't connect imaginatively with the material, what signs did you miss? This is not about blaming yourself: it's about preparing yourself to notice those signs next time around. Did you have a thorough, open-ended discussion with the writer about your, and their, vision for the story, or did you just take for granted that they'd do a good job? Have that discussion next time, and be sure you have a shared vision before an agreement is signed.

Business: Assuming that the writer is a professional, in the job because of their writing ability, the problem started with your brief. Take your share of the blame, figure out what you omitted to specify, salvage anything you can and make sure the writer is clear on what you need. Provide examples, if possible. And make your brief clearer next time.

Rule 2: Ask questions

Rule 2, Ask questions, covers everything that is not praise—in other words, anything that's not working for you as a reader. Remember: it's not your job to fix the book. It's your job to focus the writer's attention on problems and spark the writer's imagination about how to address them.

As an editor, I feel more confident if I don't expect myself to know the solution to every problem. As a writer, I am far more energized by being asked to think about my work in a new way than by being told what to do.

The purpose of asking questions is not to get answers. Questions give the writer ideas. Prompted by your question, the writer may come up with an alternative plot event or character motivation, a clearer or different chain of argument or narrative, perhaps even an entirely different way of telling the story. Your question may help the writer articulate something that's obvious to them but that isn't at all obvious to you.

I don't mean that you have to laboriously phrase every remark as a question. I mean that you should keep an open mind. If you speak from a position of "I know," you put yourself in an authoritative, even oppositional, role in relation to the writer. If you speak from a position of "I don't know," you ally yourself with the writer, who also doesn't know. If they knew how to fix what's wrong, they'd have fixed it already.

Asking good questions is somewhere between a skill and an art. You will certainly get better at it with practice. The best questions come from an imaginative engagement with the story or the subject matter, along with some background knowledge, which will differ according to what kind of writing you're working on and the intended audience.

A nonfiction book—including science, history, etc.—aimed at a specialist audience requires a specialist editor, whereas a book aimed at the general reader does not. If you are reasonably well educated and something isn't clear to you, you can assume it won't be clear to most readers; pose your questions to the writer from that perspective.

Talking with the writer

Editorial discussion is best conducted in person, or at least by phone. When you allow for back-and-forth, you are creating an environment in which good ideas can be born.

Some writers prefer to receive broad editorial notes in advance, so that they have a basis for the discussion. Usually this is the best plan if you'll be meeting by phone. But don't deliver notes from on high and expect the writer to go away and satisfy them. This makes the writer feel like a drudge, which smothers creativity.

Even if you're a film producer who has hired a writer to adapt a property you own or have optioned, you'll get a better result if you respect the writer's authorship. You'll never know the story as intimately as the writer does; they've taken it apart and examined the clockwork. They almost certainly have more to offer than what's currently on the page. Respecting the writer means that you're respecting your own judgment in hiring them.

Set a time for discussion when you've got at least an hour to spare. Make it as soon as possible, before your memory of what you read starts to cloud over.

Be aware that the writer will be feeling vulnerable; however much a writer wants feedback, it's always a bit frightening. So *always start with praise.* If the main purpose of the work has been achieved, say so. Then go to your most powerful responses: what you see as the biggest issues. Keep critical comments personal: I feel this, I think this, I'm confused about this. Phrase them as your responses, not objective judgments. A writer who values your taste and judgment will take them seriously. A writer who doesn't know you yet will be more impressed by your taste and judgment if you don't make yourself out to be an authority. Follow up your responses with questions that might clarify the underlying issue or spark a new idea. (More on what these questions might be below.) Leaving a criticism hanging in the air makes the writer feel stranded, as if they're supposed to know what to do—which most likely, right after hearing it, they don't.

You are a team exploring possibilities in search of the best solution, which may not even be on the table yet. If you say, "You need a car chase here," and the writer says, "I think that's wrong," your conversation is on the verge of becoming an argument. A writer who's been around the block a few times may rescue the situation by asking, "Why do you say that?" but often they'll just write off your suggestion as misguided and discount all your other suggestions, which may be better than this one.

In fact, your suggestion may not actually have been misguided; it was just misconveyed. You felt that the story needed a shot in the arm, and you suggested giving it one. As I said above, it would have been better if you'd stopped after diagnosing the problem, before you came up with a solution, but it doesn't always work that way. Sometimes it just seems obvious that a car chase is what's needed! If you present the idea beginning with the words "What if"—"What if there was a car chase here?"—you invite the writer to consider a possibility. That's always better than telling them what to do. If they disagree, they don't have to feel that they're fighting you. So don't insist. Turn the conversation to the reasons why that idea presented itself to you. You'll find further guidance on this in the following sections.

If you have a specific solution, remember that it might not be the best one. There's no way of telling at the present moment. I usually say something like, "This may not be a good idea, but what if there was a car chase here?" The writer may have already tried that solution and it didn't work. They may be viscerally opposed to it, perhaps because it's a cliché. They may love it and be thrilled that you gave it to them. Or—best-case scenario—your idea sparks a better one, which will come to the writer as you're talking. If you stay attached to your solution, you'll be putting an obstacle in the way of the writer's imagination. And the writer's imagination is why you're both here to begin with.

When you talk with a writer, don't feel that all issues

have to be solved by the time you stand up. You are not leaving the writer with a to-do list (at least, not in the early stages of editing). Your goal is to leave them with ideas to try out and explore—and, perhaps, a few things they can easily fix. Don't be afraid to point out niggly little issues. It feels good to be able to fix a few things quickly.

Not all writers really want to have this kind of discussion—even if they thought they did. You may find the writer is touchy and resistant to suggestions. They're not helping themselves in the long run, but it's their work and their choice. You can try to crack the writer's overly vigilant defenses by making them feel safe; praise will be your best tool. But you may have no choice other than to gracefully back away.

MAKING NOTES AS YOU READ

To be a good editor or a useful informal reader, you must read with full attention. You're not reading for your own amusement or just occupying your brain until you fall asleep. Set aside your reading time and make it as continuous as possible, with minimal distractions.

Read in a comfortable chair, not at a desk. Even though you are not being casual about your reading, you want to replicate the sense of enjoyment you feel when you settle down with a good book. You want your responses to be those of an authentic reader, albeit one who is more conscious than most readers of what those responses are.

Make quick notes wherever you feel strongly. If I'm working on hard copy, I write in the margin. If I'm reading on screen, I add comment boxes or take notes on a piece of scrap paper.

Here are some examples of useful notes:

> I don't get it.
> I'm lost/confused.
> This is slow.
> I don't care.
> No!
> Am I supposed to know something else in order to understand this?
> Why is this here?
> You said that already.
> Why is he/she doing that?
> Enough already.
> Who cares?

Note your positive responses, too. The writer needs to know what's working. I scrawl things like:

> Wow
> Hah!
> Gripping
> Brilliant
> I love this

Sometimes I just put an exclamation mark. (Avoid check marks; it takes the writer back to their school days.) Whatever thought springs to your mind is fine. You don't need to do this on every page, or even every few pages—just wherever something particularly strikes you.

This is what the writer needs to know: where you're gripped, where you're laughing or crying, where you're losing interest, where you're not convinced, where you're confused or baffled or lost.

Before you talk to the writer, ask yourself questions. Try and identify what underlying issues caused any negative responses. If you've thought of solutions, backtrack: what underlying issues are those solutions trying to solve?

Frequently, different readers have different responses to the same underlying issue. One person may feel confused while another may feel bored; one may think something should be expanded (they've jumped to a solution) while another thinks it should be deleted (they've jumped to the opposite solution). You'll be more helpful to the writer if you can identify why the writing lost its grip on you.

The next section describes issues relevant to all kinds of writing. The section that follows it gives guidance on what to look for in specific kinds of writing.

GENERAL ISSUES TO CONSIDER

A word of warning: always start from your immediate responses as you read. Use the topics below as prompts to clarify the issues underlying your responses rather than as lenses through which to analyze the writing.

Trust

In nonfiction, we trust the writer to understand the subject. In fiction, we trust the writer to know every aspect of the world in which the story takes place. If a reader loses trust in the writer, the whole deal is off.

You may find yourself thinking, as you read, "I don't believe this." First of all, distinguish between facts and assertions. If something is factually wrong—let's say, the Second World War began in 1938—and the writer doesn't simply thank you for the correction and move on, ask if they are disputing the fact: should the Second World War be thought of as having begun in 1938? If so, the argument for this version of history needs to be clarified. If a fictional story contradicts reality—let's say a character drives from Los Angeles to Catalina Island—the writer may be giving subtle clues that the story isn't taking place in the world we know (maybe there's been such an extreme drought that Catalina is now connected to the mainland). If you didn't get this, the clues are too subtle. Once a reader thinks "No!" it's hard to win them back.

You're allowed to disagree with assertions (for example, socialism is the best form of government)—but this isn't your book. Your job is to help the writer make *their* argument, *their* narrative, as strong as it can be. If you feel an assertion isn't convincing, encourage the writer to substantiate it. Is the evidence weak or absent? Is the line of argument fuzzy? If this is a historical narrative, are the cultural and political conditions of the time clear? Your counter-argument is extremely valuable as long as you aren't trying to win the battle.

Fiction requires a suspension of disbelief. To put it another way, disbelief hangs over every fictional story like the blade of a guillotine. Anything is possible in fiction, but if it doesn't accord with reality the writer needs to set clear parameters for their fictional world. In George Orwell's *Animal Farm* and Richard Adams's *Watership Down*, for instance, it's established immediately that animals have thoughts and speech, but in a book I read recently, a horse had a thought in the middle of an otherwise realistic scene. This was jarring, and for a moment I lost trust in the writer. Fortunately it was a one-time occurrence and easily fixed.

Anachronisms and misplacements have the same effect. A Civil War colonel shouldn't use the 24-hour clock in dialogue (it struck a bum note in a novel I was editing, so I looked it up: the 24-hour clock came into use during the First World War). A sound shouldn't be compared to the rattle of a train if the character hearing it has never heard a train. Even if these things aren't noticed consciously by a reader, they contribute to a sense that the writer's imaginative grasp of the story's world is shaky—which destabilizes the story unfolding within it.

My favorite example of this comes from a West Texas cowboy friend of mine. He was reading an award-winning novel by a revered author, and when the West Texas cowboy in the novel opened a gate, my friend closed the book. As he told me later, "No real cowboy opens a gate like that."

Novelists, memoirists, historians and biographers can fall into the trap of shallowness by skating over events that can't be explained or by not allowing for contradictory motivations, emotions and behavior. But trust doesn't require that the writer be able to explain everything. Nobody has yet been able to explain human nature. In fact, trust requires that the writer not pretend to be able to explain it.

It's as if the writer has a bank account—call it a trust account. Withdrawals can be made, but not too many, and not too big. Every reader does the math differently. Too many breaches of credibility and the account goes broke.

Tone

You may find yourself thinking that you don't like the writer very much, or that you don't feel comfortable in their company. If it's not a problem of trust, it's a problem of tone.

Experienced writers have found their voice, but beginning writers may still be struggling with this. As writers, we want to sound authoritative. But we don't want to sound like know-alls.

Nonfiction writers need to have a clear idea of their average reader's level of general knowledge so as not to be talking down to them or talking over their heads. Their tone must also be appropriate to the subject matter. Maybe you feel that the writer is being too jokey or too somber. Maybe you sense a superficiality, a writer who is unwilling to face the uncomfortable depths of their material. Maybe an important subject is being treated in too casual and slangy a tone. Or does the writing sound pompous, as if the writer is showing off how intelligent they are? Does the writer seem callous, lacking compassion for people affected by the events being described or for the characters being tormented by the plot they devised?

Memoir is particularly treacherous territory when it comes to tone. The voice may be so raw and intimate that it makes you uneasy, as if you're reading someone's private journal. Conversely, the story can feel self-conscious and self-serving. The writer is trotting out the version of the story they've settled on—frequently one in which they're either the victim or the hero—or they're judging their earlier self and making sure the reader understands that they're now older and wiser. A writer who tries to make the reader think well of them will usually produce the opposite effect.

In fiction and memoir, the more the writing surprises the writer, the fresher and truer it will be. The playwright Arthur Miller said, "I cannot write anything that I understand too well. If I know what something means to me, if I have already come to the end of it as an experience, I can't write it because it seems a twice-told tale." If what you're reading feels predictable or predetermined, this is probably the reason why. Ask the writer what surprised them about the story. If the answer is "Nothing," your task is to help them find new dimensions in it. Locate moments when a character could have made a different choice and prompt the writer to find new insights into why the story unfolded as it did.

A good way to bring freshness to a familiar story, or a portrait of someone you know well, is to do a 10-minute timed writing exercise starting from the prompts "I don't remember" or "What I don't know is . . ." Avoid giving the impression that you, as a reader or editor, see yourself as a writing teacher, but if you have built up a good rapport with the writer you might suggest this.

Tone can be one of the hardest things to get right. Point out a few places where the problem is most acute and offer suggestions. Could the writer set boundaries on their authoritativeness or make allowances for disagreement? Could the language be less or more measured, colloquial or humorous? Could the writer show more acceptance of complexity, more openness to the mysteries of life and human nature?

Pacing

Are you feeling bored, wishing the writer would just get on with it? Or gasping for breath as you attempt to keep up?

In nonfiction, a slow pace may result from a circuitous line of argument. If this is the case, ask the writer to make the argument to you verbally and help them streamline it. Now they have a template with which to streamline the writing. The equivalent of this in fiction is a predictable or meandering plot. Other problems might be too much description or detail, overexplaining, scenes in which nothing really happens or which have no consequences, or characters—whether imagined or historical—that don't elicit sympathy.

If, instead, the story feels hectic, like a cartoon, the writer is rushing from scene to scene, or point to point, without allowing time for the reader to develop an intellectual or emotional understanding of what's going on. Depending on the book, you might suggest more elucidation of the logical connection between one point and the next, scene-setting with details that illuminate a character's mental or emotional state, more depiction of a character's thoughts, or a more detailed breakdown of the action and its ramifications.

Digression and repetition are the most common culprits in too slow a pace. Perhaps your notes say, "Relevance?" or "We know." Bear in mind that what seems to be digressive might not be; the writer may be taking the relevance of the material for granted, or it may just be in the wrong place. Often you think you see digression, but you don't.

Repetition can present the opposite problem: you don't see it, but it's there and it's making the pace slow to a crawl. Perhaps the same concept has been presented multiple times, dressed in different words. In a fictional story, more than one scene may be having the same effect on character or plot.

Don't jump to the conclusion that digressive or repetitive material should be cut. Just point it out, by asking questions like "Why is this here?" or "How is this different from p. x?" Let the writer decide which way of presenting the concept, or which scene, or which phrase they prefer—or how they might differentiate them.

Narrative line

All books, stories and screenplays have a narrative line of some kind. Think of a narrative as a chain made up of links: something happens, which causes something else to happen, which causes the next thing. That's a plot.

Science writing often recounts the chain by which knowledge is acquired: understanding this phenomenon poses a question, which when answered poses the next question, and so on. In good polemical writing, each premise builds on the previous one. Grant proposals and annual reports are often structured around a vision of purpose or an account of goals achieved.

If you feel confused or lost as you're reading something, the narrative line has broken down or become obscured. Trace back and find the place where you started to feel yourself losing your sense of security as a reader. It's somewhere before you made your first note. Ask the writer to explain to you the narrative line from this point to the point where you made the note. Together you'll figure out what's gone awry. Could explanation or background be added—perhaps even earlier than the section you're discussing? Could the focus be confined more tightly to one storyline or line of argument? Could the chain of cause and effect, or question and answer, be clearer?

It may be that the material is muddled. It all makes sense, but you're not seeing how it all adds up. Your note may say, "This is jumping around" or "going in circles." A writer who has been working on a book for a long time and has a lot to say often finds it hard to see the forest for the trees. At times like this, your fresh eye is invaluable. Ask the writer, if it's not obvious, what point they're making or what aspect of the subject they're explaining in each section. You may need to go paragraph by paragraph and assess whether material is in the right place.

I once edited a book in which material, down to the sentence level, moved among five different chapters.

In fiction, problems with narrative line often stem from too many plotlines or characters. A good rule of thumb is to have no more than seven characters that require an emotional response from the reader. Many beginning writers don't know this. Could the writer create more differentiation between primary and secondary characters, or thin out the cast list? Maybe the central plotline could become more prominent. Is there actually a central plotline holding everything together, which begins at the start of the novel or story and ends at the end, or do beginning and ending bear little relation to each other?

Beginnings and endings

The opening of a piece of writing should grab your attention. It might raise a question in your mind, intrigue you with surprising information, draw you into a character's life at a critical moment, or transport you to another time and place. It's useful to think of the beginning of a story as a point from which there is no turning back. That gives an inbuilt sense of momentum. The ending should leave the reader with the sense of a journey completed, questions answered, a new understanding of our world or how human beings operate.

Finding the right beginning can be extremely difficult. It's not uncommon for a writer of fiction or memoir to discover the structure of the story only after they've completed a full draft, or more than one, or for a historian to try out many different openings. So, feeling a lack of focus or a sense of meandering at the beginning of a piece of writing can actually be a good sign: the writer is, like Arthur Miller, discovering the story in the writing.

I worked on my memoir *Love Child* for over a year before I figured out where it should start. I tried chronological beginnings: my mother's life before I was born, my conception and birth, my earliest memory. When I was finally able to answer the question "What is this story about?" with confidence—"It's about a girl who, after losing her mother in a car crash, pulls together an unorthodox family out of the pieces left behind"—I could see that the story started at the moment when I was told that my mother was dead.

Life is a continuum. A good story beginning focuses on a moment that sets change into motion. A good ending freeze-frames on a moment of completion or new possibility. Another way to think of this is in terms of equilibrium: a story begins when an equilibrium is disturbed and ends when a new equilibrium—however temporary—is established. By this I do not mean "happily ever after," since the new equilibrium may be precarious or even qualitatively worse than the equilibrium at the story's start. What matters is that the disturbance of the original equilibrium has been settled.

Endings are often a question of rhythm, which is hard to quantify intellectually. Once the climax of the story has been resolved, how much more is needed—or how little can the writer get away with—in order to leave the reader with a feeling of satisfaction?

Chapter endings are also very important. They should be moments of intense potential that propel the reader into the next chapter.

A slow beginning may be the result of the writer talking for a few sentences, or a few paragraphs, or a few pages, about why they're writing the book or article (known as throat-clearing). Or the writer may be easing themselves into the story with too much scene-setting or background information. Big chunks of description or backstory (what happened before the equilibrium was disturbed and the story was set in motion) slow the pace wherever they come. Ask the writer, "Is this necessary?" Don't assume it should be cut. Some of it may find a place later on.

Sometimes I will read a piece of writing and wonder why I'm reading it. The prose is good, the subject matter should be interesting, but for some reason I don't care. Usually this is because it's starting in the wrong place. If you feel this, ask the writer to tell you briefly why they're writing it. What point do they want to make? What's fascinating about the material? They'll be able to see for themselves what hooks you. That's what should go at the beginning.

In a novel, memoir or biography, a weak opening may also be due to an unlikable main character. A reader who doesn't feel an emotional connection will stop reading unless something else compels their attention. If we cannot follow this character with affection or sympathy, can we follow them with awe or amazement at what they're capable of? If an emotional connection can't be achieved in the first page or two, could the story open with narrative suspense?

Completeness

This is one of the most elusive considerations, because it's about noticing what's absent rather than what's there on the page.

Perhaps you feel dissatisfied or short-changed, but you don't know why. It might be obvious that something is missing, or you may just have a sense that there's something lacking and you don't know what. That's fine; you don't need to know what. Tell the writer how you feel and start asking questions.

Sometimes you might have no inkling that something is missing. This book is an example: in the section that deals with specific kinds of writing, there was no mention of children's books until about two weeks before the text was finalized. For nine months, I didn't notice the gap.

When reading a work of history, you might ask yourself whether all the major groups are represented: women, minorities, the less powerful social classes, the losing side of the battle. Is the narrative of events—however well told—superficial, or does it explore the effects of those events? A work of science might present fascinating facts but draw no inferences from them, or fail to discuss the ramifications of new knowledge. If you're reading a recipe or some other form of instruction, have you been told everything you need to know?

If the work you're reading is fiction or memoir, is the point of view so limited that the main character is taking up all the space? Do you understand why this story is happening? Did you get a full picture of the story's world? Did the story resolve the questions it posed, leaving things poised in a new equilibrium?

Style

No editor can make a lively writer out of a plodding one, but good line editing can improve the prose. If you're an informal reader, don't take this problem on. Arm yourself with praise for whatever you think is strongest about the content—maybe the plot or the writer's knowledge of the subject—and suggest that the prose could be livelier, or tighter, or more personal. Be aware that this will be a tough thing for the writer to hear; they're likely to jump straight to "You're saying I'm a bad writer." Your answer to that is that you're just offering a personal opinion based on your feelings as you read, not an objective judgment.

If the writer responds positively to your comment on their prose style, they may ask for your help. Don't get talked into line editing an entire book! It's a huge job. If you feel confident of your skill—and only if you do—offer to work on a page or two. When you give it back, don't say, "This is what I mean" or anything that conveys that you've fixed it. Say something neutral like, "See what you think of this." Hopefully you will inspire the writer to bring the rest of the material up to this standard—and beyond.

In a screenplay, the equivalent of leaden prose is leaden dialogue, which is usually the result of a simplistic conception of character. You could suggest that the writer pull together some actor friends and have them improvise. If the stage directions seem overly detailed, suggest the author read some published screenplays for guidance. You'd be amazed at how many aspiring screenwriters have never read a professional screenplay.

Excess material

When repetitions, digressions and extraneous material have been identified during the editing process, the writer may agree that cuts will make the work stronger but feel upset about the wasted effort that went into the deleted passages. Few writers believe that every word they write is gold, yet many writers take the need for cuts as a criticism of their writing ability.

The screenwriting guru Robert McKee has a dictum: 90% of what you write is research. By "research," he doesn't just mean the accumulation of facts; he means anything that helps you know your story and characters better. Many people who hear this feel that 90/10 is too extreme a proportion, and that may be true for them, but for some writers the reality is even more extreme. Either way, it's not the proportion that matters. What matters is that a finished draft comes into being, however much "research" has to be generated along the way.

Writing that 90%—or whatever the proportion is—is necessary in order to obtain the usable 10%. The work wasn't wasted. In the 90% ideas are developed and clarified, characters are explored, points of view and plot possibilities are tried out. If you feel that passages in what you're reading should end up as part of the 90%—that is, they may not belong in the final draft—look for phrases and details that you'd be sorry to lose. If, after discussion, the writer decides to cut the material, you can suggest that those nuggets be worked in elsewhere.

WHAT TO LOOK FOR IN SPECIFIC KINDS OF WRITING

An understanding of the requirements of various kinds of writing makes your feedback as an early reader or editor more useful. As this book is about how to edit rather than about how to write, the following material gives only a very cursory overview. You'll find some recommendations for further reading at the end of this book.

Fiction and memoir (including plays and screenplays)

These are stories of human lives. (Okay, the characters might be animals or robots, but even so they will have human traits if the writer wants us to care about them.) Though it is nonfiction, memoir tends to be structured in the way a novel would be structured. Fiction tends to be more tightly plotted, memoir can be looser and more digressive, but both tell a cohesive story.

First, let's differentiate memoir from autobiography. An autobiography is the record of a life to date, written by someone who is already well known. We read an autobiography because we are curious about the life this person has led. Its narrative thread is almost always chronological and is centered on whatever made the autobiographer famous. A memoir, on the other hand, is a narrative tale drawn from the writer's life, with a storyline that builds to a climax and resolution. The writer need not be famous. The story need not begin when the life does, nor need it end at the present day. We read memoirs for the same reason we read novels: because we are endlessly fascinated by why human beings do what we do, and how we deal with the constant challenges of life.

If you'd like to develop your understanding of story, I recommend two books: Robert McKee's *Story* and John Truby's *The Anatomy of Story*. McKee and Truby have differing ideas of the components of story, but both present powerful arguments for what makes a story strong. (Both come from the world of screenwriting. Books on screenwriting are useful for all storytellers, since screenwriting is story with the prose—the "telling"—stripped away.) Even if you're working on material that is unorthodox or experimental, understanding the theory of story gives you an anchor. It's the equivalent of academic drawing for artists: the basic form from which innovation departs. I once went to an exhibition of Picasso's early sketchbooks: case after case of academic drawings. Before he started painting bodies broken down into planes, he made sure he knew how to draw one faithfully.

I find it useful to think of a story as the disturbance of an equilibrium and the sequence of events that leads to a new equilibrium being established. The beginning poses a question of some kind, which is resolved by the end. Even if there isn't an obvious quest, the main characters are taking actions to bring about their desired outcomes, and that is what creates the plot.

Writers of fiction and memoir tend to start from either character or plot. Starting with plot can lead to flat, predictable characters; starting with character can lead to a weak or meandering plot as well as to wispy secondary characters. As I've said before, don't leap to the conclusion that these are signs of bad writing; they may simply be signs of a non-final draft. It's normal that when you start building from one side, the other side lags behind.

When a writer bases a story on their own life experience, they may have a hard time seeing what happened from anyone else's point of view. It can also be difficult to see where the story begins and ends, since we live our lives as a continuum. If it isn't clear what the story is actually about, ask the writer to tell you. An answer that goes, "and then this happened, and then this happened," is not a story; it's a succession of events. In a strong story, one thing causes the next, with unpredictable incursions disrupting and twisting the chain. And there is a change from beginning to ending: we close the book knowing that things can never again be as they were.

Setups and payoffs

Anton Chekhov famously said that if a gun is hanging on the wall in the first act of a play, it should be fired before the play ends. The corollary of this is that if you're going to fire a gun at the climax, it should be hanging on the wall earlier. In other words, don't make dramatic promises you don't mean to keep, and don't have big events come out of nowhere.

The gun hanging on the wall is a setup. The gun being fired is the payoff. Payoffs without setups feel random. Setups without payoffs make the reader feel short-changed. Layering in these connections across time gives depth and believability to the writing.

Let's say a character has to kill their horse. The emotional impact will be greater if there was an earlier moment when either this character or a different character connected with the horse, or if we've already seen how vital the horse is to someone's survival. Or let's say there's a moment in a story when a character feels completely abandoned. This could be set up by previous, less extreme moments of abandonment and/or moments when the character believes they are safe from abandonment.

Exposition as ammunition
This is my other favorite Robert McKee dictum. Exposition is information about the past, or anything else you need to know in order to understand what's going on. It becomes ammunition when revealing it has consequences.

Information without impact is dull. It should be given at a time when it propels the plot forward, illuminates a hidden or mysterious aspect of character or is charged with emotional content.

Exposition that isn't ammunition tends to fall into one of two categories:

Dialogue in which characters tell each other stuff they both already know. Real people don't talk this way. Dialogue that's motivated only by the writer's desire to get some information across to the reader is dead on the page. Trying to disguise exposition with phrases like "Mom, have you forgotten that . . ." is cheating, and it's easily spotted.

Weightless facts. If you are told a fact about a character and you think, "So what?" the fact has no weight. For example, in a book of history I edited, it was mentioned that a character had a phobia of insects. Just the bald fact. I asked the writer whether this phobia had consequences—because if it didn't, there was no need even to mention it. We explored possible scenes in which the phobia could be triggered without great consequence, which would set up a later scene in which severe consequences resulted from the phobia.

Let's assume that it is necessary for the reader to know a certain piece of information. The question then is, where in the story does it become crucial? Where does it face a character with a dramatic choice? Where could it be used by a character in an attempt to bring about some desired result? Where might it be revealed under pressure because the choice not to reveal it is even worse, or because it's become impossible to suppress? Where does it impel a character too powerfully to resist? Where does knowledge of it turn a character's world upside down?

The classic example is when Darth Vader tells Luke Skywalker, "I am your father." We could have been told that at any point during the first *Star Wars* film. Instead, the information was withheld until the climax, with shattering impact.

Character

Characters that feel predictable are acting according to the demands of the plot rather than according to their own desires and needs. This may sound absurd to you: if they weren't, the plot would be different. What this means is that characters must take on a life beyond the necessities of the plot, so that the reader feels that they are creating the plot rather than the other way around.

Dialogue in which characters say exactly what they need to say in order to advance the plot, telling one another plainly what they think and feel and want, is the most obvious sign of this problem. (For example: "Hi, Alice, I was really hoping that you'd call me tonight.") Screenwriters call this kind of dialogue on-the-nose. When a real person speaks, they are trying to bring about some result; they are trying to affect or influence whoever they're speaking to, and perhaps other listeners as well. Thoughts, emotions, needs and desires both conscious and unconscious run beneath the words. This is called subtext.

There are two basic questions to ask about any character: What do they want? and, What do they need? The two may be the same, but in stories with psychological depth they are not. Either or both may change in the course of the story. The character may not be conscious of their need or may think they need something quite different. The character will have an overarching desire, a defining psychological need, but may want or need something very specific in a given scene.

I find that whenever plot or character motivation in

a novel, memoir or biography feels fuzzy, asking these two questions helps to clarify things. Every character will always be taking steps toward what they want—in film speak, this is known as the desire line—and doing things driven by need.

Problems may arise when the most prominent character in a story is not structurally the protagonist—the character whose choices and actions are driving the plot forward. Individual scenes may be terrific, but the story as a whole sputters. You may feel a sense of meandering, imbalance or even confusion in the plot. You may feel frustrated that the most prominent character doesn't seem to do much. You may wonder why all these people are even in the same book.

The protagonist of a story doesn't have to be likable as long as they're capable of eliciting a reader's empathy. Do you have a sense of why they want what they want, or the need that's driving them? If you don't give a damn about them, explore with the writer how those elements might be brought into sharper focus.

Antagonists are characters who try to prevent the protagonist from getting what he or she wants. Do these characters have goals of their own, or are they merely thwarting the protagonist? If a villain seems to be acting villainously only because the plot demands it, ask the writer what values are driving this character. If the character was telling the story from their own perspective, what would that sound like? All human beings do what they consider right according to their own necessities and moral code.

What to look for in specific kinds of writing—

The stronger an antagonist is, the better. It's a misconception to think that a hero seems strong because they easily overcome opposition. The stronger the opposition, the greater the victory.

We hear a lot about "three-dimensional" characters. Just "dimensional" would be a better word. Believable characters, like all human beings, are a complex mixture of positive and negative traits. They suffer inner conflicts. If a character seems flat or boring, it's probably because you have no sense of their inner conflicts. Your questions can help the writer figure out what those inner conflicts might be. What makes the character feel guilty, embarrassed, resentful, jealous, envious or angry? Under what circumstances do they feel justified or unjustified in these emotions? What do they hold sacred? What wrong that's been done to them are they trying to make right? What outside the plot is going on in their lives?

Everyone has a story: a family or lack of family, a childhood, formative experiences, superstitions, things and people they love and hate. A minor character becomes more than a mere functionary if they are given just a hint of any of these. A quick fix is to give them a quirk, like a Bond villain's cat. It's not enough to elicit empathy in a reader or viewer, but at least it gives the character some interest.

Service characters—such as a taxi driver fulfilling a role demanded by the plot—don't need to be dimensional. However, if a service character feels too cursory, ask the writer how that person would recount the incident later. Seeing them as the hero of their own story often generates a detail or a line of dialogue that gives the character a stamp of individuality.

Overt psychologizing takes the reader out of a story. Psychology should stay in the subtext. Some writers try to "explain" a character with backstory: for example, she can't hold down a job because her mother was an alcoholic. Human nature can't be explained with a "because." Human beings aren't machines that can be reverse-engineered; that's why we're so endlessly fascinating. Some daughters of alcoholics may be neurotic, or workaholic, or alcoholics themselves; others become therapists or Buddhists or bartenders or anything else under the sun. Ask the writer why the earlier experience propelled the character in a certain direction. The more specific the character's journey, the more believable and sympathetic the character.

Be careful with the question "Why is the character doing this?" It can prod the writer into coming up with a recipe-type explanation. The results will be better if your discussion of the question is exploratory and open-ended. If you don't believe a character's action or motivation, ask yourself whether your response is actual disbelief or just an unwillingness to accept something—for example, that a character you like takes an action that you find appalling. Ask why the character thought that was the right thing to do. Did the character consider alternative actions before settling on this one? Are there mitigating circumstances? Do other characters in the story share your disbelief?

Perhaps later story events will clarify the action. That's not a bad thing. Resolving the kind of disbelief that's really shock with later understanding is one of the pleasures of story. However, it's vital that even though your trust in the writer has been jolted, you're still "in" the story. If you feel like tossing the book aside, let the writer know that for you, at least, the shock was too intense. Could a setup be added earlier to bring the shock back to the believable side of the line?

Conflict
Drama is conflict.

Conflict, in this sense, doesn't mean fighting and arguing. At its most basic, it is the opposition of the antagonist(s) to what the protagonist is trying to achieve. The story will have a primary zone of conflict: for example, personal moral conflict, family conflict, spiritual anguish, outlaws versus the law, warfare, the conflict of hope against fate, of humans against the natural world or of the individual against the tide of history. A very strong scene that takes place outside the story's primary zone of conflict can feel out of place.

This is not to say that there can only be one kind of conflict in a story—just that one is primary. Layers of conflict add depth. Whatever is going on in the main plot, there's likely to be some inner conflict within the protagonist and perhaps other characters too. If a group of characters are in conflict against some outer force or entity, there is likely to be conflict among them. The sense of imbalance arises if this secondary conflict is more powerful or interesting than the conflict driving the main plot.

The stakes

Conflict is only interesting because of what's at stake. Is it clear what the consequences will be if the protagonist succeeds or fails, and are those consequences big enough for us to care about?

Think of a poker game. A penny-ante game may be fun to play but it's boring to watch. A game with millions at stake is compelling. In a compelling story, whether fiction or nonfiction, the stakes are high: for better or worse the lives of the characters, the tide of history, the fate of mankind or the earth or the galaxy will be changed.

Drama is choice. A choice with little or no consequence—shall I eat an apple or a pear?—has nothing at stake. A choice between good and bad—shall I eat this good apple or that apple which I know to be poisoned?—is interesting only when the unexpected choice is made. Though the consequences of eating the poisoned apple are potentially serious, the stakes are low: I lose nothing by choosing the good and rejecting the bad. But if there is good and bad on both sides of the choice, the stakes are higher and so is the tension. Do I save the cash under the mattress or my dying mother's treasured photo album from the burning building—or do I protect my life and let them both burn? The character loses something whichever way they choose, and we see what they are willing to lose, or risk, in order to gain, or save, what they value more. A high-stakes choice defines character and also sparks empathy, since we feel the magnitude of what the character is risking, or sacrificing, in making the choice.

But if the stakes are high at the beginning of a story, it

What to look for in specific kinds of writing—

has nowhere to go. In good story construction, the stakes rise: obstructions are harder to overcome, consequences more severe, sacrifices more meaningful. If the stakes don't rise, or if the choice a character makes brings them no nearer to or further from their goal, the plot sags and the reader loses interest.

For simplicity, we can categorize stakes into life, liberty and the pursuit of happiness. Rising stakes within the same category make for a coherent and compelling story. Is a character in danger of a painful fall, then a disabling accident, then of death? Are they in a bad marriage which they could leave, and subsequently find themselves in a situation that they really can't escape? Is a romantic setback the precursor to genuine heartbreak? The stakes should be at their highest at the climax of the story: the ultimate victory or defeat, the rise or collapse of empire, the life-defining decision, the do-or-die moment, the acquisition of vital wisdom at great cost.

A common problem in storylines taken from history or from the writer's own experience is the sense that the story is dragging on; it just won't end. This occurs either because the writer hasn't correctly identified the climax of the story or hasn't built up to it with rising stakes. Explore with the writer what the most important stakes in the story are, and where they are highest. That's the climax. The writer may choose to include some kind of coda after the climactic resolution so that the reader closes the book with the sense of a new equilibrium, but it's a good idea to keep it minimal. In story terms, we're done.

If there's superfluous material after the climax, don't jump to the conclusion that it should be cut. It may simply be in the wrong place. Could it come earlier, as a character's hopes or fears for the future? Or could the writer take what's powerful about this material and work it in to an earlier, different plot event?

Should it be a novel or a memoir?
Sometimes the writer can't decide. Here are some useful questions to ask:

Could anybody sue you for libel? If so, the story had better be presented as fiction, though if the person is easily identifiable the problem persists. Disguise is necessary.

Are you going to hurt anybody you don't want to hurt if you publish this as a memoir? If so, fictionalize it. People may still recognize themselves, but you'd be amazed at how often they don't. And, as above, you have opportunities for disguise.

Are you comfortable publicly taking ownership of this story as having happened to you? If not, go with fiction.

Are the true events of the story hard to believe? Making it a memoir asserts their reality.

Does the story come to a satisfying conclusion, or does it fizzle out? This is a frequent problem with stories taken from life. There are two ways to go here. Either the editor can press the writer to dig deeper inside and find some probably hard-won, possibly uncomfortable resolution of events; or the writer may prefer to use the real-life story as a basis for fiction, and invent a dramatically satisfying ending—which may require inventing new plot along the way as well. The editor and writer can toss ideas back and forth as they explore how the premise could turn out differently.

If you can in good conscience tell a true story that has an intriguing beginning, a middle with twists and turns and rising stakes, and a satisfying ending, my advice is to make it a memoir.

Fiction and memoir: Praise

- Plot: Is it exciting, unexpected, suspenseful, illuminating?
- Character: Do you care about a character—ideally, more than one?
- Sense of place: Do you get a strong sense of the buildings, landscape, social dynamics?
- Style: Does the prose draw you in with pleasing rhythms, lively word choices, unexpected juxtapositions?
- Particular scenes: Were you moved to tears, laughter, fear, relief or another emotion?
- Moments that feel particularly real: Especially when they make you see a familiar aspect of life in a new way.
- Satisfaction: Did you feel a sense of completion when you finished the book? Did it make you think differently about your own life or other people?

Fiction: Questions to ask yourself as a reader

- Do you believe the world and the characters?
  The most bizarre science fiction is believable as long as the rules of the world are clear. The most peculiar characters are believable if their motivations are recognizable and strong.
- Do you care?
  We read stories because as humans we enjoy making emotional connections. Do you feel a shared humanity, even with nonhuman characters? Robots, animals and replicants engage us when they show recognizable human traits and emotions: courage, compassion, greed, envy, hunger for power, love, kindness, generosity, loneliness and so on.
- Is the story coherent?
  Could you follow it clearly? Does the equilibrium established at the end reflect the disturbance of equilibrium at the beginning? Or does the story just seem to stop?
- Do you feel empathy for more than just the central character?
  Is the writer making everyone else wrong in order to make themselves (in the shape of the protagonist) right? In other words, does it feel self-serving?
- Are the settings vivid? Can you imagine what it would be like to live these people's lives?
- Does the story feel fresh, or do you feel like you've read it before?

What to look for in specific kinds of writing—

Memoir: Questions to ask yourself as a reader
- First of all, is this piece of writing appropriate for a reader? Writing can be excellent therapy, but that doesn't mean it should be read by anyone else. Raw, spilling-your-guts writing is personal exploration, not communication.
- Do you believe the writer is being honest, or giving a biased version of events in order to show themselves in the best possible (or worst possible) light?
- Do you feel the writer is trotting out a well-worn version of the story, or have they gone back into it imaginatively and made it fresh?
- Does the writer give other characters their due, or do they seem to think theirs is the only legitimate point of view on the story's events? Is it an exercise in self-justification?
- If the author is fictionalizing to some extent, e.g. with dialogue, is it within the bounds of faithfulness to what really occurred, or could they be accused of not telling the truth?

Screenplays and stage plays: more questions
There are many books that set out the specific technical and dramatic guidelines for these formats. If you are an informal reader, you cannot be expected to provide professional-level script editing or dramaturgy, so it's fine to limit your response to how the story struck you. Practical advice for industry professionals can be found on pp. 67–71.

- Is it exciting or intriguing?
- Is it clearly told?
- Do you care about the characters?
- Do you think audiences would want to see this?
- Is it relevant to the current moment?
- Does it feel fresh, or like something you've seen before?

Books for young readers

Non-adult books divide into three categories: picture books, middle grade (ages 8–12) and young adult (or YA, ages 13–18). It's essential that the writer is clear about what readership they're targeting. Rules for this genre are stricter than for any other and are constantly changing, so what was acceptable or unacceptable five years ago may be the opposite today. The first question for the writer is, have you read lots of recently published books in the category you're working in? The second is, have you given your book to readers of the target age?

Writers of children's books must avoid being didactic. Picture books often have lessons, but they shouldn't feel like lessons. The older the reader, the more resistant to being lectured they will be. Any lesson should be deeply embedded in the story. Though a happy ending isn't compulsory, a book for young readers that doesn't end on at least a hopeful note may not get professionally published.

Picture books: There's a strict word limit. The writer should know what that is, and observe it. Most publishers choose the illustrator, but if you have been given pictures as well as text keep in mind that the words shouldn't just

What to look for in specific kinds of writing—

copy the pictures, and the pictures should include more than what the words say. Parents have to read these books repeatedly, so don't underestimate how good the quality of the writing should be. Even small children respond more enthusiastically to lively writing than to writing that's plodding or predictable. You're looking for freshness, surprise, charm and richness of imagination. These qualities are hard to describe, but you know them when you see them.

Middle grade: Intriguing story/character questions must be raised in the reader's mind immediately the book starts. It's got to be a page-turner. Even if it's a quiet book about everyday life, the reader should be in suspense about how the kid in the book is going to deal with various situations. These books usually have short chapters and less complicated emotions than you will find in books for older readers.

Young adult: Voice is everything. Emotions are complex, and depth of emotion is vital. The language, thoughts and worldview of the main character must feel real and recognizable to the teenager reading the book. If the story is contemporary, the characters must be authentic to the world we live in. If it's historical, fantasy or science fiction, the writer must strike a balance between what a reader today can identify with and what's appropriate to the era or setting.

- Is the book appropriate, in language and subject matter, for the reader age it's intended for?
- Do you feel that the writer is fully inside the mind and body of the kid in the book?

- Is there an obvious lesson that might feel didactic to a reader?
- Is the writer talking down to the reader?
- Do the characters accurately reflect the diversity (in ethnicity, religion, gender, sexual orientation, economic circumstances, physical and mental abilities, etc.) of the world we live in?
- Is the writer writing about what they know, or do the characters feel borrowed?

Nonfiction

The most important elements in any work of nonfiction are clarity and narrative drive. Different considerations apply to the various genres. You will be able easily to adapt these considerations into questions for the writer.

History

A historical narrative should be more than a catalogue of events. A good historian portrays the effects of events on society, the earth and individual people, and shows how they resonate (or not) today.

- Why is it important to tell this story?
- Does the writer have a viewpoint on the events (e.g., admiring, condemnatory) and is it supported?
- Is the story clear, both chronologically and as a chain of cause and effect?
- Is the setting vivid? Can you imagine what it was like to live at this time?
- Do you understand who the main actors are

What to look for in specific kinds of writing—

and what is driving them?
- Do you understand the effects of their actions on the society at large?
- Does the book make you feel the consequences of historical events on a human scale?
- Is the book thoroughly researched, or does the writer's knowledge feel shallow?
- Are the research sources properly notated and credited?
- Is there a need for this book, or is it simply repeating what other books have already covered? What's new about it?

Polemic

Books that make an argument are usually about politics or current affairs, popular or intellectual culture. You might disagree with the premise or conclusion of a polemical book, but as an editor or informal reader your job is to take it on its own terms and help the writer make it as strong as it can be. If you can't do that because you disagree too profoundly, remove yourself from the project.

Repetitiveness is a common danger in polemical writing. The writer wants to hammer home a point, and often they're unwilling to cut repetition. But hectoring people is not the best way to convince them. Tell the writer if you feel you're being hectored and explore ways to add charm to the argument—maybe with a clever turn of phrase or an anecdote to lighten things up.

- Why is it important to make this argument?
- Has the writer convinced you? Have you changed

your mind on the subject as a result of reading the book? If you were inclined to agree with the writer before you began, have you gained new insights that have strengthened your belief in the validity of the argument?
- Even if the writer hasn't convinced you, is the logic of the argument tight?
- Does the argument build, or does it meander or go in circles?
- Are assertions grounded in fact and supported by notes?
- Is there a call to action? A diatribe about what's wrong with no vision of how to fix it makes for dismal reading.

Science

Science books frequently have compelling storylines. When one thing is discovered or explained, what question does that provoke? And when that question is answered, what is the next question? This is how science itself progresses, and it's a good way to structure a book on the subject. A strong science writer explores the conflict between the old paradigm and the new knowledge, as well as between competing theories or competing scientists.

Some academics feel that it's unseemly to write with too personal a voice or to show their enthusiasm for the subject. This makes the writing dry. The best science writing is alive with the excitement of discovery.

- Did you understand the science? And why it's worth understanding?

- Is the book abstract, or has the author shown how the science affects human experience?
- Is there a clear line of progression from simpler concepts to difficult? Or, if the book is structured episodically, with a different aspect or application of the science discussed chapter by chapter, do you feel that you have a comprehensive picture?
- Is there a need for this book, or is it simply repeating what other books have already covered? What's new?

Cooking, gardening, other how-to books

The most important considerations are clarity and completeness, followed by passion. Try a few recipes or projects to make sure the instructions are clear and complete but don't feel that you have to try them all. A careful writer will make sure that all instructions have been beta-tested before going to print.

Many books of this kind include some passages of memoir, usually in an introduction and often in introductory paragraphs to individual recipes or projects. This is where the writer conveys their passion for the activity and perhaps tells the reader how they discovered it. Even a short section of memoir should feel like a little story. Refer to the fiction/memoir section above.

- Do you feel inspired by the writer's passion to try some of these projects?
- Are instructions clear, complete and in the right order?
- Are technical terms given consistently?

For example, oven temperature is always either Fahrenheit or Celsius, measurements are either metric or imperial, the Latin names of plants are included or omitted.
- Would it be helpful to include appendices such as a glossary, a list of tools needed or places to purchase specialist items?
- Is there a need for this book, or is it simply repeating what other books have already covered? What's new?

Self-help

Self-help is a genre that overlaps with many others: health, cooking, philosophy, science. It usually contains elements of memoir, as most writers of self-help books are speaking from their own experience. Clarity, trust and tone are the most important considerations. The reader has to understand clearly what problems the information in the book solves, they must trust that the writer knows what they're talking about, and they must feel safe, respected and inspired to follow the writer's advice. A self-help writer who hectors, blames or talks down to the reader is not an appealing mentor.

- Is the writer talking to the reader in a tone that's personal, honest, authoritative and sympathetic?
- Is the value of what the book recommends clear?
- Are the problem and the intended outcome clearly described?
- Is the advice grounded in science, statistics and the experience of many people, not just the writer?

- Are the steps in the process clearly differentiated and in the correct order?
- Is there a troubleshooting section: advice for when things don't go according to plan?
- Is there supplemental material to support and engage the reader? For example, charts to fill out, questionnaires to answer, blank pages to journal on.
- Is there a need for this book, or is it simply repeating what other books have already covered? What's new?

Magazine articles

The subject matter of a magazine article will fall under one or more of the categories above. But the form brings up some specific considerations.

- Is there something new or thought-provoking in the piece?
- Is it lively to read?
- Does it feel relevant to the moment?
- Does the beginning grab your attention and hold it?
- Is the content appropriate to the length? Does the piece feel padded, or too compressed to be understood easily? If so, could the subject either be expanded or restricted?

Business/nonprofit documents

The primary considerations for documents such as grant proposals and annual reports are clarity and authoritativeness (exemplified by specific, measurable goals and statistics), followed by passion. An effective document conveys belief in your mission, your product or your service. Passion is what convinces a funding organization or an investor to buy in. It is what makes you stand out from the competent competition.

Look always for stories that show the value of your organization to people's lives. Look for moments of drama (e.g., a sudden leap in earnings, recognition from the UN) and highlight them. Look for places to show how your company's mission statement guides the company's actions.

Poetry

Poetry editing is a very specialized field, almost always undertaken by other poets. If a friend asks you to be a reader for their poetry and this is out of your comfort zone, say so. Encourage them to join a poetry writing group or find a class.

FOR PROFESSIONALS

I have organized the advice below according to which professional should find it most useful, though there is a great deal of overlap. Informal readers should find this section useful as well.

Book/magazine editors and literary agents

In this section I will refer to "the author" instead of "the writer" as that is the term used by professional publishers.

First of all, you'll want to establish the method

by which you'll be working. On hard copy or in a Word document using Track Changes and comment boxes? (Word is the standard program in professional use.) Will you be editing chapter by chapter or waiting for the full manuscript? Take time to build rapport with the author on technicalities such as this, which should be pretty neutral ground. You will make deposits into your trust account by agreeing to the author's preferences wherever possible and expressing encouragement and enthusiasm about working with them.

Know when your authors are due to deliver and check whether they'll be on time, so that you can set aside reading time. Please don't ignore a newly delivered manuscript, letting weeks or even months go by, as some editors do. Acknowledge receipt with thanks, and if you won't have time to read it very soon tell the author when you plan to read it. Stick to the reading date you gave.

When you begin the editing process, expect some defensiveness, or at the very least a level of wariness. The author doesn't yet know whether your judgment is to be trusted or whether your comments, however good, will come across harshly. Many authors are primed for disappointment, disagreement and even open conflict.

It's your job to convince the author that you are on their team.

Think of yourself as the author's ally in bringing their work to its full potential. You are not their teacher or their boss—even if you commissioned them. Blanket directives will put an author's back up.

Avoid giving the impression that you're setting yourself up as a kind of judge. Sounding as if you believe yourself to be an arbiter of what good writing is, rather than offering a personal response—though an educated one—will result in the writer distrusting you or resenting you. They have to listen to your opinion; you want them to respect it. I write comments such as "I'm not following you here" and even "Sorry if I'm being dim, but I don't understand" (fairly frequent when I'm editing science books). The more personal and nonjudgmental my tone is with an author, the more editing they'll accept and the more work they're willing to do.

Don't be inscrutable. Explain why you're making suggestions, even if you think the reason should be obvious. Once you and the author have come to know each other, you can take shortcuts. In the early days, err on the side of too much explanation and too many question marks.

Don't use red pen! For many people, it recalls school and strict teachers and sends them back to their twelve-year-old selves, which is not helpful. This is unlikely to come up much since most editing is done online, but if you find yourself working on hard copy choose green, blue, regular pencil, anything but red.

Don't embed big-picture thoughts in comment boxes. Write them out in a covering letter.

When you send editorial notes to an author, always end with an invitation to discuss them further.

And remember, always lead with praise.

Line editing

When a book has big-picture issues that need resolving, sort them out first. That way, you won't have wasted time on material that ends up being cut or rewritten.

Once you're at the line editing stage, you don't have to present every change as a question or a suggestion. Still, avoid giving the impression that you're imposing yourself or being dictatorial. I add comment boxes saying things like "Suggest moving as shown," "Is this tighter?," "See what you think," or "OK with you?" If you're editing on hard copy, put a circled question mark in the margin. Explain briefly why you made any change that isn't really obvious (e.g., repeated word or phrase, murky syntax).

If I make a change that I feel is a judgment call, I flag it with "or something like that," if necessary explaining why the original seems inadequate. If I am asking for a change instead of making one, I will write something like "Avoid 'referring/reference' in the same sentence?" or "This seems a bit awkward—are you happy with it?"

There is no fixed rule for what you should flag. If the file is close to immaculate, you can assume that the author has looked carefully at everything, down to the commas. In a case like this, I will flag even an inserted comma (which isn't easily visible in Track Changes) with a comment box saying "OK?" But don't overload the file with comment boxes. It's tedious for the author to answer "OK?" a thousand times. If many changes fit into a category, spell that out in your covering letter (e.g., "Many sentences start with 'It seems that . . .' so I've rephrased throughout"). You rarely need to explain why you're fixing bad grammar.

Some further things to look for when line editing:

- Repetition of a thought, an emotion, a fact, an argument.
- Blathering on, saying the same thing over again in different words.
- Clunky rhythm or strange word order.
- Jargon.
- Vagueness.
- Mixed metaphors. If the author doesn't want to lose one, separate them—into different paragraphs, if possible.
- Repetitive rhythm: not enough variation in sentence length or structure.
- Overuse of particular words or phrases.
- Overstatement and tautology: e.g., "bloody slaughter."
- Clichés.
- Throat-clearing: "nevertheless," "therefore," "however," etc.
- Adverbs. Often you can find a livelier verb that doesn't need modifying. If there's no way around it, look for an adverb that's unexpected.
- Anachronisms. Check anything that seems out of place. For example, that Civil War novel mentioned on p. 24 included kudzu, Shangri-La and taxicabs (all incorrect for the period). A work of history complained of the lack of X-ray machines in a hospital in the 1880s (they hadn't been invented yet). Another novel used the word "guerrilla" to

describe warfare in 1869—which actually turned out to be correct. The term came into use during the Peninsular War (who knew?). Because it caught me up I flagged it, and the author decided to remove it on the grounds that if it seemed anachronistic to me it would seem anachronistic to other readers as well.
- Consistent chronology, especially in novels. Are characters aging at the same rate as the years are passing? Is weather appropriate to the season? Are trees and flowers blooming or fading at the right time of year?

Don't over-edit! I will be the one to tell you that it's better to do too little than too much. Don't strangle the author's voice. Don't assume that something that's provocative and funny is automatically offensive and should be removed; the author may want to ruffle a few feathers. Don't sacrifice power of expression to punctiliousness of grammar. Don't homogenize (unless the magazine, or series, demands it). Let the author be their unique self.

Asking the author to expand

A scene is cursory; an argument should be expanded; a magazine article isn't long enough. When you ask a writer to add material, give them guidance by asking questions. What in particular do you feel is missing? What further ideas would you like them to address? Your questions spark ideas, and they also demonstrate that you have engaged with the story or the subject matter.

Wrangling the writer

You are an editor; if you'd wanted to be a therapist, you'd be one. However, you are going to need some therapist's skills. People who create something out of nothing feel vulnerable, and frequently they identify themselves with their work: "If this piece of writing isn't good enough, that means I'm not a good enough writer." Much of the advice in this book is designed to counteract that problem, but it won't work for every writer. Be patient and keep your tone positive and collaborative.

Some authors are nervous about letting go. They start anticipating all the possible criticisms of their book, and keep making trivial changes. At a certain point, probably when the production schedule demands it, you will have to tell them that the time for edits is over. If you can, say, "You wrote a good book." Those are the words that all writers are longing to hear.

The converse is when you feel there is more work to be done but the author is tapped out. You have two choices: with the author's permission you could do the work, if that's even possible, or you will just have to accept that this is as far as the author can go.

Some authors are just plain difficult: defensive, dictatorial, short-tempered, dismissive of editorial input. If you think an author is being unreasonable, call in reinforcements: the editorial director of your imprint or the editor-in-chief of the magazine. If the author was commissioned to write something specific, whether an article or a contribution to another author's book, the person who did the commissioning is the one to decide how editing should progress. It's rare that an author in these circumstances can successfully refuse to be edited.

If you are an editor working with commissioned writers, you are in a position similar to that of a film/TV development executive, so please read the following section.

Film/TV producers and development executives

I'm going to assume that if you're an industry professional you've read at least some of the many excellent books on screenplay structure. What those books don't tell you is how best to work with the writer. I have been a producer and a development executive as well as a screenwriter, so I have sympathy with all sides.

Commissioning a screenplay is an inherently stressful situation. There's a lot of money at stake, and you are not in control of the result. You are at the writer's mercy. You are also answerable to the source of the money that's paying the writer: a senior producer, studio executive or investor of some kind. You are caught in the middle.

The common instinct is to assert as much control as possible. This is counterproductive.

Your best starting place is a place of trust. This writer is a good writer; that's why they were hired. They have talent, insight, storytelling sense, professional chops. They know what they're doing and will deliver on time. As the months elapse, you might discover that you can't trust a writer to be as professional as they should be—this comes under the heading of "shit happens." But don't start the process operating from that fear. If you do, you're likely to create what you fear.

The number one mistake development executives and producers make is being bossy. Don't ask to see pages unless you're willing to take no for an answer. Not all writers start at the beginning and work through to the end. Often a writer will work out of sequence or will expect to rework earlier scenes after later ones are written. Asking a writer to deliver something they're not yet satisfied with is a recipe for trouble.

If, for whatever reason, it is vital that you see the writer's work in progress (maybe you have a demanding financier), let the writer know in advance and make sure they are willing to work this way. That demanding financier is, at heart, also operating from a place of fear, so try to find a way of assuaging their fear and promoting trust in the writer. Set up a meeting between them if you can, at which they both can explain their vision for the screenplay and perhaps describe certain scenes. Maybe the writer will agree to a weekly phone call to discuss progress. If the writer is not willing to agree even to this and your demanding superior is immovable, you may need to find a different writer. It's better to know up-front that a working relationship won't work than to discover this after money and time are spent.

Contact the writer a few weeks before the delivery date and ask if they're going to deliver on time. If the date is crucial, make sure the writer knows that at the start. Delivery a week or two late is not usually a big deal. The writer is probably keen to deliver too—their next payment depends on it.

For professionals—

Remind your producers/financiers that the writer is about to deliver. Allow a week or so of wiggle room, in case the writer is late. Read the screenplay promptly and with care. Don't make the writer wait weeks. You knew the delivery date, you checked on progress; it's only respectful to schedule in a few hours of reading time.

Ask the writer whether they'd prefer individual responses or combined notes. You may not be able to deliver the writer's preference, but at least you've shown the writer that you have an understanding of the process. As a writer, I much prefer individual responses; that way I can triangulate among them (see p. 81). Combined notes tend to be both a compromise among viewpoints and a random collection of solutions which may or may not be workable, or not all workable together.

Film/TV executives are prone to trying to fix a writer's work, rather than stopping after they've identified a problem and opening up a discussion. Be aware that this is not necessarily the most productive strategy, though you will probably be unable to stop other members of the team from employing it. Do your best to understand what problems their proposed solutions are trying to solve, and differentiate the contributions of various people when you discuss combined notes with the writer.

Try to avoid the situation in which multiple members of the producing team deliver their responses at once, in person. It seems more efficient, but more than two voices easily becomes a barrage, especially when those people are wedded to the solutions they've come up with. Real pros are used to this, but less experienced writers can't help getting defensive.

There is an understandable drive for script meetings to end with solutions, because script development is a team effort and investment is on the line. But solutions stifle possibilities, and solutions decided upon before the writer is even consulted tend to be predictable and derivative. This is why so many films tread the same ground. Sparking the writer's imagination will produce a better screenplay in the end—that's why the writer is writing it, not the producers. You may be able to cajole your producers into letting a meeting end without solutions by asking the writer to send further thoughts within a few days.

I have a "10 pages back" rule for screenplays. The place where the problem becomes apparent is not the place to start trying to fix it. Around 10 pages back is where the problem started to form.

- Something wasn't set up.
- A character made a choice that sent the narrative into a dead end.
- A step is missing: the stakes have risen too drastically.
- The plot is feeling repetitive because the stakes aren't rising: the writer will have to devise more danger, put more at risk.
- We don't care about the character: the writer will have to find a private moment earlier to open a window onto the character's hope, fear, desire or need.

- There's too much backstory: even if it should be cut, explore with the writer how it can be worked into other scenes.

A collaborative, exploratory discussion with the writer will generate ideas about how to solve problems. A critical attitude will get you a defensive writer with a shut-down imagination.

Taking the line, "We're paying for this, you're supposed to get it right," will in the end cost more.

Business/nonprofit executives

It's taken for granted these days that all business materials should be professionally designed. Yet it's amazing how many are not professionally copyedited or proofread. I frequently notice spelling, punctuation and grammatical mistakes in promotional materials, websites and newsletters. Not everyone will notice these consciously, but if there are more than a scattered few, your potential clients, customers and investors will have a sense of sloppiness and unprofessionalism. Was it really worth saving a few hundred dollars?

Do not rely on your writer to produce error-free copy. Very good writers are often shaky on spelling, punctuation and grammar. The more someone works on a piece of writing, the less likely they are to see mistakes. When you already know what something says, it's hard to see typos. Hire a professional copyeditor and proofreader for everything that goes out of house.

FOR WRITERS
Editing yourself
Remember to view things that aren't working not as flaws but as signs that this is still a work in progress. That this piece of writing exists at all is a triumph. Your immediate goal is to get to the next draft. Don't think you have to solve every issue in one fell swoop.

When should you edit? Whenever is best for you. Many writers edit what they wrote the previous day and then continue with some momentum. They build a book the way you'd build a wall: brick upon brick. I find that these are usually experienced, confident writers. The rest of us are less sure of ourselves, and the more we can take down the pressure to be good by considering what we write as just "material" or a "rough draft," the easier it is to fill a blank page with words.

I find that it doesn't help to "edit as I write." Once I start thinking that what I write ought to be good, my critical mind suffocates my imagination. Originality disappears. I'm one of those writers who makes a big mess and then cleans it up. I write nonsequentially, not caring whether what I write is "good" and expecting that at least 90% of it will end up as what Robert McKee calls research. Only when I have the bulk of the story on paper do I dare read it over and start to edit.

Since I write in disconnected chunks, my first step is to join them up. I start wherever I sense a progression, a chain of cause and effect. I often know where the story will end, but I'm less sure where it begins. So I will be looking for what the equilibrium might have been before the story got going, and the moment of disturbance from which there is no turning back. I may be a few drafts in before I really settle on where the story starts.

There's no rule about whether you should line edit first or do the big stuff. If you can't focus on the storyline and characters because you're distracted by rough, messy writing, tidy it up. But don't get bogged down in style at this point: just get the prose clear enough so that you can see the content. Once the narrative is solidly in place you can worry about scene-setting, description, turn of phrase or details that make the writing sparkle.

I find that too much material is easier to deal with than too little. It's easier for me to see what shouldn't be there than what's missing. If 10% of what you write is worthy of the final draft, you're doing brilliantly—but you still have to write the other 90%. And it's not just math. When you've written something and cut it out, its ghost prompts you to make changes elsewhere that infuse the writing with subtext.

The screenwriter and novelist William Goldman has a famous dictum: "Kill your darlings." If you find that you're emotionally attached to something that you know in your heart of hearts isn't working—or which multiple readers find confusing, distracting or unbelievable—that's a "darling." Darlings will haul the center of gravity away from where it should be; you're forcing the material to accommodate them. See what happens if you cut that scene, that character, that event. It's not lost! Maybe you'll use it in your next piece of writing—or the one after that.

Don't worry if your writing, when you first read it over, is wordy, repetitive, overwrought, confused. It's not supposed to be good, that's why it's called an early draft.

The actual words
The simplest words are usually the strongest. Only use a long word if it's giving more information than a shorter one—and I don't mean information about how smart the writer is.

A famous rule of good writing is to remove adverbs. Adverbs can be useful in an early draft, as a kind of shorthand reminder of how you're imagining the action of a scene; that way you don't have to lose your momentum searching for the exact word. But English is a rich language: it's full of near-synonyms with slightly different meanings and connotations. You can usually get the sense of the adverb, and more, into a different verb. For example: "He walked slowly." This says only that he didn't walk fast. Did he saunter, amble, dawdle, drag himself, meander, edge, creep, inch, plod? You're adding emotional subtext: he's pleased with himself; he's carefree; he's lazy; he's unwilling; he's aimless; he's afraid; he's dangerous; he's uncertain; he's tired; he's bored.

Read your work aloud
The last stage in editing your own work should be reading it aloud. Yes, the whole thing, from beginning to end. Do I hear you protesting that this will take way too long? But think about it: how much time have you spent working on this already? Five, or ten, or twenty more hours is virtually nothing by comparison.

For writers—

Set aside blocks of time as continuous as your schedule allows. Find a place where you're not self-conscious about being overheard. This reading is just for you.

When you read silently, the words just roll along. You wrote them so you know what to expect, and guess what? Your expectations are met. Reading aloud adds a dimension of objectivity. You will hear plodding or hasty rhythms, repetition and overused words. You may also feel little twinges of falseness when you hit something pretentious or inauthentic.

It's even more helpful to read your work aloud with full emotional and intellectual engagement, as if you were reading for an audience. Stand. Project your voice with commitment and passion. Convey to the empty room, as powerfully as you can, the meaning of the words you're reading. Now you are not just listening to the words; you are feeling them.

When you load your writing with its full freight of meaning, you know viscerally when something feels wrong. It will make you wince and you'll be highly motivated to revise that section. You're also more likely to notice things that don't make sense, as well as gaps and kinks in the logical chain by which one sentence follows another and one paragraph follows another. You feel the disconnect when you're not actually saying exactly what you want to say.

Don't be tempted to include listeners at this stage. Their reactions will be biased by how good you are at reading aloud and by their own familiarity with being read aloud to. Some people aren't accustomed to it and get fidgety; others love audiobooks and are used to professional readers—in other words, to a standard that you are not trained to achieve. Either way, you won't get accurate feedback on your writing.

Too many writers discount the importance of being good at reading aloud. It's a valuable and underused tool in the editing process, and after your work is published it will be a critical tool in building your fan base. The Twice 5 Miles guide *How to Read for an Audience* was written for you.

Writing groups

Writing groups are most helpful if they keep you on track with your writing. They're also a great source of informal readers and editors. You can offer to act as editor for writers whose work you like, and with luck you will forge long-lasting reciprocal relationships. It's a gift to any writer to have readers whose judgment they trust.

Some groups focus on writing exercises, usually of 10 or 20 minutes' duration. (I prefer 10; it doesn't give you enough time to stop and think, so what comes out tends to be fresher and more surprising.) You can use these exercises to develop material for your serious project or simply to hone your skills. The good thing about short exercises is that they tend to silence the inner critic. How can you possibly write something good in 10 minutes? It's an absurd expectation, so it's not hard to drop it. What you're looking for in this raw material are moments when the writing pops: little bursts of energy. You'll know it when you hear it. If you achieved that just once, well done! You've created something out of nothing. And if you didn't, big deal, you only wasted 10 minutes.

In other groups, writers read from their ongoing projects and are given feedback. Don't feel that you have to go this route. It's fine to keep your serious work private until it's at a more finished stage.

Creative writing courses

I do not think criticism should be a spectator sport. The setup in which a writer reads their work aloud and stands there while the rest of the class comments on it— ostensibly with the goal of helping the writer, but more frequently with the goal of impressing the teacher— reminds me of the struggle sessions of the Chinese Cultural Revolution. You don't have to put yourself through this. What's more, classes such as these tend to produce writers who sound like a lot of other writers. Guess why: it's harder for the class to criticize writing that's just like everybody else's.

Good creative writing courses and MFA programs are conscious of their responsibility to nurture individual voices, not turn out cookie-cutter writers. The best way to decide whether a course is right for you is to talk to people who have taken it and read the work of alumni. If that work feels like they could all have been written by the same alumnus, look elsewhere.

Finding a good editor

This is an exciting time to be a writer. Agents and publishers no longer control what books are available to the public. Self-publishing is easy and inexpensive.

However, books that haven't been professionally published often feel like amateur work. It doesn't have to be that way! Get a professional to design the cover and the interior typography. Get a professional to copyedit and proofread. And before you get to that stage, find a good editor.

This is a good tactic even if you hope to be taken on by a professional publishing house. Lists are dwindling, and the number of editors working on them is dwindling faster. The days when editors like Maxwell Perkins or Marjorie Villiers spotted potential in a writer and spent months or years working to develop that writer's talent—or edited a book so heavily as to virtually rewrite it—are over. You will have one chance to impress an agent, publisher or magazine editor, so you need your work to be as good as it can be.

Many people advertise editing services, but often those who style themselves editors are in fact copyeditors. You may need them—but later. Ask writer friends for recommendations. Join online forums. Interview potential editors to discover if they've worked with writers in your genre and what they think constitutes a good thriller/polemic/memoir/work of history/YA novel. Ask them to explain their working method. You're looking for some version of "Praise and ask questions." If the answer is more like, "I'm going to tell you what's wrong with your writing and how to fix it," move on. If they seem to be breaching a previous client's confidentiality, move on. You should be able to expect the same discretion of an editor that you would expect of a doctor. (In Hollywood, writers who thoroughly overhaul screenplays are actually known as script doctors.)

If your work is in good shape but the spelling, punctuation or grammar are iffy, get a basic copyedit before you send it out. You want to look professional. The gatekeepers at literary agencies, publishers and magazines are usually overworked; they don't want to deal with amateurs.

Asking friends and family to read your work

Perhaps you don't have the money to hire an editor or can't find one you trust, or you simply want feedback before you start to spend money. Many writers ask friends and family to read their work. Yet this situation is fraught with pitfalls. People who love you don't want to hurt you, and they will inevitably feel put on the spot by being asked to give an honest opinion. On the other hand, they want to help. So they will be nervous about saying either yes or no.

How do you navigate this?

Choose the right readers

I highly recommend that you DO NOT ask family members or very close friends to read your work until it is finished or very nearly finished. There's usually too much emotional charge. In the best case, this person really wants to tell you it's great. Sometimes they will deliberately omit to mention problems or weaknesses they noticed; sometimes their desire to like your work will blind them to problems or weaknesses. Either way, the response is not much use to you. "It's really great!" tells you nothing. Sure, you can press them and hopefully you'll discover that they really did think it was great, and why, and that will boost your confidence and energy. But save this until you know from other readers that the work is in good shape.

In the worst-case scenario, there's an undercurrent of competitiveness. Jealousies and resentments may not be conscious, yet they fester among family members and friends, as well as among colleagues and fellow students. They come out in unpredictable ways, and they will compromise an objective reading of your work.

Another drawback is that someone who knows you very well may be unable to help looking for aspects of you, your life or people you both know in your writing—particularly if they don't yet think of you as a writer. This too will compromise an objective reading.

Your best readers are people you have a cordial relationship with—cordial enough to ask for the favor of taking time out of their lives to help you—but who aren't so close that their personal feelings will get in the way of an honest response. Your absolute best readers are people who write too; that way, you can reciprocate. It's not just a matter of tit-for-tat, though that's important when you're asking for hours of someone's time. It's beneficial to have an exchange in which neither person is the judge. You take turns in the roles of criticizer and criticized. When the reader knows that they will be on the receiving end at some point in the future, or they have been already, they're more likely to be empathetic and gentle as they share their responses.

Be aware of how much you're asking in terms of time. Be grateful to the people who will do this for you!

Give your readers instructions
I say to my readers, "Please tell me your honest reactions as you read. I'm not looking for ideas, but feel free to tell me any ideas you think might be useful. What I really need to know is what you loved, what you hated, what made you laugh or cry, anywhere you felt bored or confused or annoyed or short-changed."

Your readers will be grateful for instructions, especially if they're not used to reading work in progress. Give or lend them this book and point them toward the final section, "For informal readers."

Don't burn too many fresh eyes on one draft
You'll only get a fresh, objective response once from each reader. If the same person reads a new draft, they can't help looking for what's changed and whether any suggestions they made were incorporated. None of this is relevant to anyone but themselves. So line up 10 or 12 readers, if you can. That gives you enough for three or four rounds of feedback. Don't use up more than three per draft. I like that number because it allows me to triangulate responses.

Triangulating readers' responses
Having multiple readers of a draft allows you to step back from individual responses and view your work in an analytical, rather than a critical, way. The more readers

who have a similar response at any given point, the more you can trust that response. Often you will find that readers focus on the same place in your writing yet have wildly differing responses. This can be disorientating and confusing.

Since your readers are reading out of a genuine desire to help, they are looking for solutions—even though you've guided them away from that. It's natural. Your task is to figure out why they are saying what they're saying, what underlying problem could have provoked these differing responses. Look back 10 pages, even 20. Problems always begin before a reader feels strongly enough to make a note.

Give your readers a time frame
It's easier for you if responses from multiple readers come in at roughly the same time. If you're circulating just one printout, you don't want it to drag on for months. So agree on a time frame before handing over the manuscript.

If someone can't read within your time frame, move on. Maybe they can be a reader on the next round.

Give your readers a hard copy if possible
It's easier for most people to read on paper than on a screen, even if they're used to a Kindle. Your book has not been professionally designed yet, so even if they get it on their tablet it won't look like an e-book. The sense of turning pages is integral to the reading experience, and you will get a more accurate response if you invest a bit of money in printing. Use 12-point type, double-spaced,

with paragraphs indented rather than separated by a line space. This is publishing industry standard.

Another advantage of a printout is that it's a visible physical object. Even though someone has agreed to read your work, they're likely to procrastinate because they're nervous. Seeing it sitting there waiting to be read will prod them.

Tell your readers whether or not you want them to write directly on the printout. If cost is an issue for you, have them write their responses on a separate sheet of paper with every comment identified by page number, so that you can use the same printout for another reader. Never give a reader a printout that's been marked up by somebody else.

FOR INFORMAL READERS

A writer friend has asked you to read their work. What do you do?

When to say no

If you think you won't be able to be objective, say so. You don't have to explain why. Maybe you feel that long-standing interpersonal dynamics will color your reactions. Maybe you're too afraid of hurting the writer's feelings. It doesn't matter whether this is because they're overly sensitive or because you are unsure of yourself; in either case, you're not the right reader for them.

If you're willing to do the writer this favor, ask how much time it will take—and expect the writer's estimate to be low. I can read a clean, double-spaced typescript at about 40 pages an hour, and I read fast. Mistakes in spelling and punctuation, tortuous grammar or laborious storytelling slow a reader down. Add on time for thinking about the book and discussing it with the writer. For a full-length novel, you may be looking at 15–20 hours. This is a big ask. You are absolutely entitled to say no, you don't have time right now. If you don't want to refuse outright, offer to read the book at a later stage. Maybe your time will be freer then.

If you're not sure you can finish the book within the writer's time frame—ask them if they don't give you one—don't agree to be a reader. The writer will be on tenterhooks awaiting your opinion, and if you have to keep putting it off they'll get anxious, you'll feel guilty, and it will become a problem between you. Figure that if you say yes, you'll be able to read the book within a week or so. If you get delayed tell the writer so, but know that they are still on tenterhooks, wondering if you've really not started or if you might be lying because you don't like it.

Set your escape hatch
You may have no idea whether your friend has any writing talent at all. This isn't a professional situation where you can rely on a certain minimum standard and a protocol for rejection. So, before you read a word, say something like, "I'll read the first 10 pages, and if I'm not responding to it I'll just stop there, because obviously I'm not the right reader for you."

(I know: repetition! It's important enough to say again.)

For informal readers—

Set aside your reading time
Devote a full afternoon, day or weekend to this task if you possibly can. Don't read a work in progress in the casual way you'd read a published book. Give it sustained attention. If you're reading 10 pages a day, you're less likely to feel involved with the story or characters and more likely to have trouble following a potentially complex plot or subject matter.

Keep your notes short
The more time you spend writing notes, the more you're taking yourself out of the flow of the book and compromising your responses. So keep them short. You can always go back and expand later.

Make sure you know whether or not the writer wants you to mark up the printout. If they do, use an exclamation mark or just a word or two where something strikes you. Remember to make your handwriting readable.

If you're not writing on the printout, a quick scrawl on a bit of scrap paper is best. Type it up later. Don't type while reading! Moving to your computer, waking it up, putting in the password, noticing that email that just came in—all of this takes you out of the book. If you're already sitting at your desk with the computer on, then you're reading in the wrong frame of mind anyway.

When you stop reading for the day, look back over your notes to make sure you know what you meant, and elaborate if necessary. If you leave it a day or two, your notes may well be as baffling to you as they will be to the writer.

Don't worry about line edits
That is, unless you see something glaringly awful. Focusing on line edits means you're not focusing on the big picture and you're no longer in the mindset of an ordinary reader. It becomes about you: how many mistakes can you spot?

The writer didn't ask you to copyedit; what the writer needs is your response to the content and impact of the writing. But if the spelling, grammar and punctuation are distractingly bad or there are lots of handwritten corrections, tell the writer that you can't provide an accurate reaction because your reading experience wasn't smooth.

Let the writer dictate the terms of discussion
The writer values your opinion; that's why they asked you to read their work. But you may find that even though the writer asked for an honest opinion, in reality they don't want to hear that their work is anything less than perfect, however sensitively you phrase it. If that's the case, just back away. Your friendship may be on the line. The writer is doing their work a disservice, but there's nothing you can do about it.

Remember the two basic rules:

Rule 1. Praise
Rule 2. Ask questions

FURTHER READING

Daniel Alarcon, ed. *The Secret Miracle: The Novelist's Handbook*. New York: Macmillan, 2010.

Lisa Cron. *Wired for Story: The Writer's Guide to Using Brain Science to Hook Readers from the Very First Sentence*. Berkeley: Ten Speed Press, 2012.

Peter Ginna, ed. *What Editors Do: The Art, Craft, and Business of Book Editing*. Chicago: University of Chicago Press, 2017.

Gerald Gross, ed. *Editors on Editing: What Writers Need to Know About What Editors Do*. New York: Grove Press, 1993.

Robert McKee. *Story: Substance, Structure, Style, and the Principles of Screenwriting.* New York: ReganBooks, 1997.

Billy Mernit. *Writing the Romantic Comedy*. New York: Harper Perennial, 2001.

Howard Mittelmark and Sandra Newman. *How Not to Write a Novel: 200 Classic Mistakes and How to Avoid Them— A Misstep-by-Misstep Guide*. New York: Harper, 2008.

Ann Patchett. "The Getaway Car." In *This Is the Story of a Happy Marriage*. New York: HarperCollins, 2013.

Linda Seger. *Making a Good Script Great*. West Hollywood, CA: Silman-James Press, 2010.

John Truby. *The Anatomy of Story: 22 Steps to Becoming a Master Storyteller*. New York: Farrar, Straus and Giroux, 2008.

This book is also available in e-book, audiobook and downloadable pdf formats. Please visit twice5miles.com for details on these and other Twice 5 Miles titles.

If you enjoyed this book, please post a review on the website of your favorite online retailer.

www.ingramcontent.com/pod-product-compliance
Lightning Source LLC
Chambersburg PA
CBHW052028290426
44112CB00014B/2425